T0197622

AuthorHouse™ UK
1663 Liberty Drive
Bloomington, IN 47403 USA
www.authorhouse.co.uk
UK TFN: 0800 0148641 (Toll Free inside the UK)
UK Local: 02036 956322 (+44 20 3695 6322 from outside the UK)

Because of the dynamic nature of the Internet, any web addresses or links contained in this book may have changed
since publication and may no longer be valid. The views expressed in this work are solely those of the author and do not
necessarily reflect the views of the publisher, and the publisher hereby disclaims any responsibility for them.

Any people depicted in stock imagery provided by Getty Images are models,
and such images are being used for illustrative purposes only.
Certain stock imagery © Getty Images.

This book is printed on acid-free paper.

ISBN: 978-1-7283-5543-6 (sc)
ISBN: 978-1-7283-5544-3 (e)

Print information available on the last page.

Published by AuthorHouse 12/16/2020

authorHOUSE®

First things first, we're going to put things straight about how my brain works. Let's take a look back at when I was younger, age 4. I just felt different from everyone else. I felt like everyone at school could get on and do their work really quickly, and I would sit at my desk fiddling with my pencils or anything I had. The next minute I would notice everyone was going out for break time, and I would have to stay in to do my work again—only to still sit there and play with anything I had. It was like a gear in my brain that just wouldn't turn. If I have no interest, there is no oil in my brain to help the gears move.

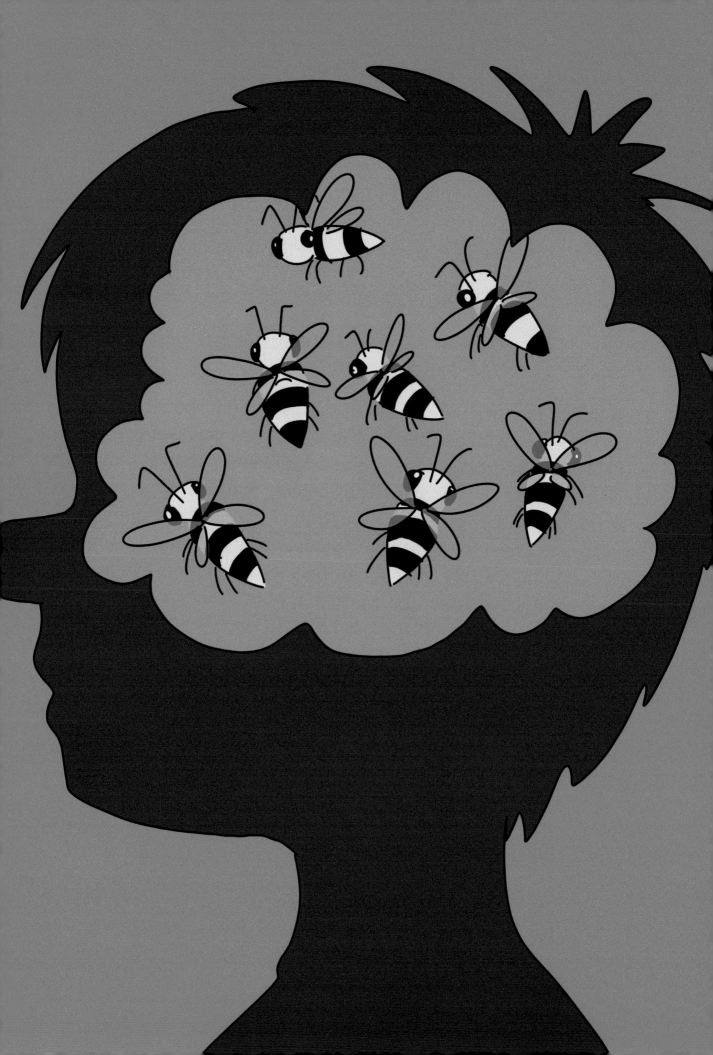

On the other hand, when I am interested, the ideas are like a swarm of invading bees, millions of ideas, and there's no brakes to stop them or keep them still, so I can't organize my thoughts.

And then there's overload—being asked to do too many things at once. It's like a huge lorry of rock arriving at the factory and being tipped onto a conveyor belt. The belt is overloaded and comes to a complete stop. This causes a total factory shutdown, and I feel like it can never be sorted without help from others.

I feel angry, sad, frustrated, confused, overloaded, misunderstood, treated unfairly and overwhelmed.

Hyperfocus is when only one thing takes over the entire brain. For me in class, it can be anything I really like or am interested in, but it's usually steam engines or thinking about one day being rich or going home. Hyperfocus can be really hard to move on from.

Then there's worry, where what starts out as one small worry gets bigger and bigger until it's absolutely ginormous, which leads to engine malfunction, water leaks (tears), steam (anger), cogs flying in different directions (destruction), pistons clanging (arguing), and red lights flashing (embarrassment).

Time to get up, time to put shoes on, time for school, time to go in, time to start work ...time this, time that. Time! Time! Time! I really don't get why everyone is telling me about time. I'm just sitting there getting relaxed, and then there's someone (again) telling me about time. Time seems to make grown-ups get cross.

"William, you have five minutes left on your PS4."

"William, you have two minutes left on your PS4."

"William, you're ten minutes over your five minutes. We don't have time for this!"

If there was just daytime and night-time, surely everyone could be more relaxed.

As for sleep, going to sleep for me is like a steam train engine. I may be told it's bedtime, but the fire can take hours to go out. Ideas go through my head like live embers dancing in the firebox; just one idea can start the fire all over again.

I lose things, and I'm not just talking about objects. I can also lose ideas. In class, I can have a really good and very important thing to say, and I've got my hand up, then the teacher is pointing to me and *whoosh*—it's gone?

I can also lose instructions.

"William, go brush your teeth, please."

"Yes, Mum." I go upstairs, put my music on, and play with my toys, no memory of having been asked to brush them until "William, have you brushed your teeth?" reminds me that's why I'm upstairs.

Then there's losing objects. Pens, pencils, coats, bags, phone—anything really. I can just look away and then they have gone. Can I find them? No, I can't.

But why can everyone else?

OK, so let's get out of my brain—it is so busy in there.

I'm ready for a PlayStation break.

Talking about how my ADHD brain is working and putting it on paper has helped me slow down and look at what happens to me every day. If you see me in school just sitting there not doing my work, maybe my gears need some oil. Tell me the instructions again—I could have lost them! *Boom!* I may have too many bees in my brain and can't sort them. My conveyor belt in the factory could be overloading and coming to a stop, maybe as I'm hyperfocusing on steam trains.

This is the point where things could go wrong. If I've been told to hurry up and do my work without the above being sorted out, this then can turn into worry, which gets bigger and bigger, and then engine malfunction! This can be seen in many ways: tears, anger, destruction, arguing or refusal to work at all. If this point is reached, it's very hard to come back from. What helps is complete removal from the situation. Break time is very important, even if that's just a walk or five minutes out of the room. I don't like getting upset, and I'm often embarrassed when I do. So please help me, as my behaviour is not a conscious decision—more a slippery slope on which I need help.

Sometimes my ADHD and dyslexia just get the better of me, but there are things that help. My one-to-one at school helps me to stay on track. She explains my work to me again if needed. Not being shouted at helps, because shouting just makes me angry and upset.

Sometimes going for a walk, when things in class are too much, helps me calm down and refocus. Having extra time to finish work helps too, and I don't mean during my break time—that just upsets me. I need to play.

Mum helps by organizing my school bag with me and remembering all the things I need for the day.

I have my dyslexia lesson once a week at school, which is made fun so I don't feel like it's work.

I have a good teacher who is understanding. My mum is really good to talk to. When I feel listened to, it helps me to let go of my worries. She gives me extra help so I can find and organize my things.

Tips for helping me.

Let me move—keeping in all that "needing to move" is so hard, and trying not to get into trouble for it can give me anxiety.

Seat me in class where I'm not easily distracted. Maybe you have things you could add to the list. We're not all the same, and even the tiniest idea could make the biggest difference.

I also get help from a place called CAMHS (Children and Adolescent Medical Health Services). I go there every few months to see a psychiatrist with my mum and dad. I get to talk about how I'm doing at school, how I'm feeling, and if I'm having any problems. That psychiatrist also gives me medication for my ADHD. I take it before school and at lunch time. The medication helps my brain to slow down the thoughts and ideas (the bees), which then helps to oil the gears, which then keeps the conveyor belt from overloading. Much less worry and frustration, so no engine malfunction. This means a much happier school day and a much happier me.

The psychiatrist also helps me with my sleep. First thing for sleep is a good routine, so no electronics an hour before bed. I have a nice warm bath and get a good book to read before bed, but sometimes even all this does not work for me. So I have medication before bed that just helps me get to sleep. It stops the embers dancing around my firebox (brain) so I can just have a quiet, restful head.

Remember, your ADHD and dyslexia can also be a super power. Look at me, I wrote a book. Hope it helps.

William (Age 9)

Unique Kind Willing to take risks

Humorous Inspiring

Loving Charming

Awesome
qualities
of
A D H D

Adventurous Creative

problem solver

Inspiring Caring

Never different bored

Lives in the moment

resourceful

Printed in the United States
By Bookmasters